Twenty to Make
Polymer Clay Bears

Birdy Heywood

Search Press

First published in Great Britain 2010

Search Press Limited
Wellwood, North Farm Road,
Tunbridge Wells, Kent TN2 3DR

Text copyright © Birdy Heywood 2010

Photographs by Debbie Patterson at
Search Press Studios

Photographs and design copyright
© Search Press Ltd 2010

ISBN: 978-1-84448-504-8

Suppliers
If you have difficulty in obtaining any of the
materials and equipment mentioned in this book,
then please visit the Search Press website for
details of suppliers: www.searchpress.com

Printed in Malaysia

*This book is dedicated to the
animals of this world.*

Contents

Introduction

All the bears in this book are easy to make if you follow the simple guidelines for dividing the clay into the correct proportions. They are all based around an easy to assemble structure. As the book progresses, I have added little tips on how to create folds and claws, and also how to position your creations to give them life and movement. A slight tilting of the head, the position of the eyes or the general pose of the bear can change its personality.

Polymer clay is a coloured modelling clay that can be baked hard using an ordinary oven. There are several polymer clays on the market to choose from, all available at good craft shops. The baking temperature of each individual polymer clay differs, so please follow the manufacturer's baking and safety guidelines. Some clays are softer than others, so choose the clay to suit your needs. There are many colours to choose from and the clay can be blended to create your own colours.

Polymer clay, unlike sugarpaste, should not be eaten. It is also advisable to use tools and utensils that will not be used for food preparation. For cake toppers such as the Birthday Bears, shown on page 17, use a simple cake display board to mount your bear on, to prevent contact with the icing.

The guidelines in this book can also be used to create the same figures out of sugarpaste or other modelling clays, but do not use glass beads for the eyes if you want to make edible bears.

Experiment with your bear making and enjoy it. Every bear will be different.

A selection of the polymer clay bears you can make using this book.

Basic proportions

These instructions are used to make the Simple Bear on page 8. Most of the other bears are based on these instructions, with minor variations.

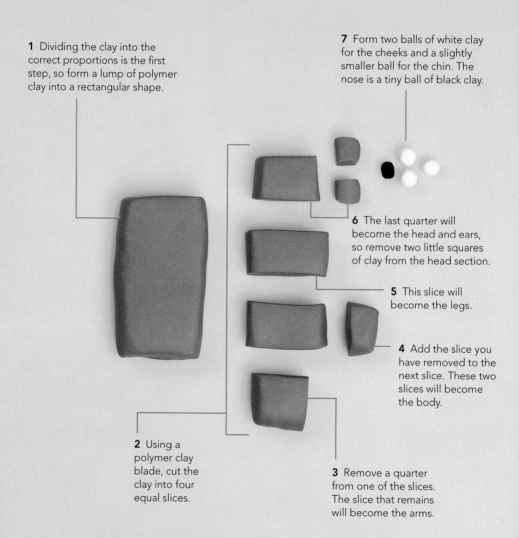

1 Dividing the clay into the correct proportions is the first step, so form a lump of polymer clay into a rectangular shape.

7 Form two balls of white clay for the cheeks and a slightly smaller ball for the chin. The nose is a tiny ball of black clay.

6 The last quarter will become the head and ears, so remove two little squares of clay from the head section.

5 This slice will become the legs.

4 Add the slice you have removed to the next slice. These two slices will become the body.

2 Using a polymer clay blade, cut the clay into four equal slices.

3 Remove a quarter from one of the slices. The slice that remains will become the arms.

Basic tools

Pasta machine

To flatten the clay. A glass roller can also be used.

Aluminium foil

For creating armatures.

Wet wipes

For cleaning hands in between using different colours.

Oven thermometer

To ensure the clay is baked at the correct temperature.

Ceramic tile

To bake the bears on. You can also use a baking tray.

Polymer clay blade

For cutting clay.

Round, square and small star cookie cutters

For top hat, mortar board and wand.

Blusher and brush

For bears' cheeks.

Knitting needle

To create eye sockets.

Wooden cocktail sticks

To create claws and folds.

Glass beads

For eyes.

Metal jump rings

For Gypsy Bear's earrings (page 34).

Scrap of lace or paper doily

For making impressions on Baby Bear's blanket (page 44).

Selection of polymer clay blocks

Simple Bear

Materials:

Half a block of brown polymer clay

A little white clay and a tiny spot of black for the nose

Two tiny glass beads for eyes

Tools:

Polymer clay blade to cut the clay

Knitting needle to create the ear holes

Half a wooden cocktail stick to support the head

A cocktail stick to insert the glass beads

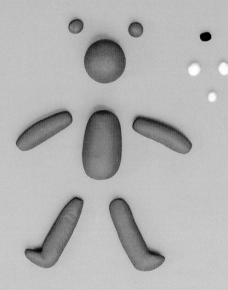

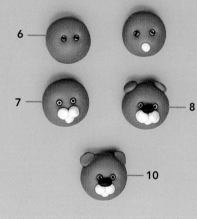

Instructions:

1 Divide the clay as shown on page 6.

2 Form the shapes as shown above.

3 Attach the legs to the body by pressing firmly, taking care not to distort the tops of the legs.

4 Attach the arms.

5 Push the blunt end of the half cocktail stick into the top of the body, leaving a little protruding, as shown (right).

6 Insert the glass beads as eyes, using the cocktail stick.

7 Add the chin followed by the cheeks as shown above.

8 Attach the little black nose.

9 Place the head firmly down on the protruding cocktail stick to attach it to the body.

10 To make the ears, press the little balls firmly on the head, then pinch them to flatten them slightly.

11 Use the knitting needle to create the ear holes.

12 Bake your bear at the recommended temperature on a ceramic tile or baking tray.

8

The Simple Bear is the basis for all the other bears in the book. He is shown here with two friends. The larger blue bear has a brown snout and a very big nose. He also has little brown matching pads on his paws, which are created by squashing tiny flattened balls of brown clay into place. He has larger ears and his eyes are closer together. The little pink bear has a tiny, round nose made from deep pink clay. Her ears have been placed further down and she holds a blanket made from flattened white clay. The claws were created using a cocktail stick to make the indentations.

Wedding Bear

Materials:

Half a block of brown polymer clay for the
body; a little lighter brown for the snout;
black for the nose and hat; mix black and
white to create grey for his tie; two shades
of pink for the bouquet and flower crown

Two glass beads for eyes

Tools:

Polymer clay blade

Knitting needle

Half a cocktail stick to support the head

Cocktail stick to support the leg, and another
to create claw impressions and flowers

Round cookie cutter for the base of hat

Pasta machine or roller

A cup to support the
bears while baking
so they don't topple

Ceramic tile

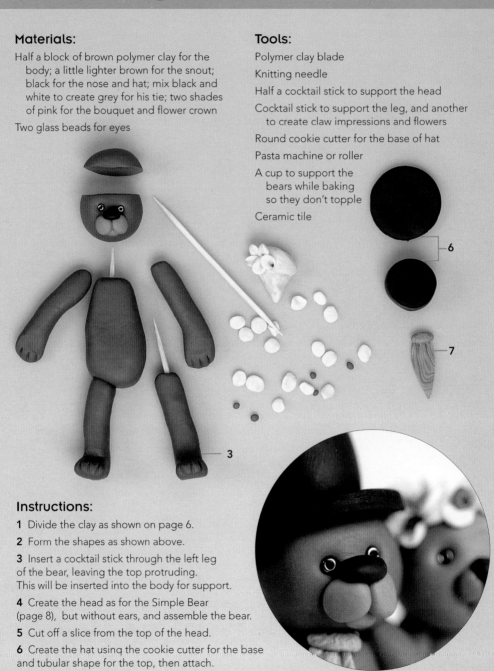

Instructions:

1 Divide the clay as shown on page 6.

2 Form the shapes as shown above.

3 Insert a cocktail stick through the left leg
of the bear, leaving the top protruding.
This will be inserted into the body for support.

4 Create the head as for the Simple Bear
(page 8), but without ears, and assemble the bear.

5 Cut off a slice from the top of the head.

6 Create the hat using the cookie cutter for the base
and tubular shape for the top, then attach.

7 Flatten some grey clay and cut out a tie, then attach it to the bear.

8 Lean him against a cup for support while he waits for his bride.

This loving couple could be made in sugarpaste to decorate a bear lover's wedding cake. The bride is assembled the same way as the groom, in a redder clay, but this time, add ears and insert the supporting cocktail stick into her right leg. Her snout is smaller and more dainty and her nose small and round.

To create her bouquet (see opposite page), form lots of small balls of pink clay, then flatten them. Form very tiny darker pink balls for the centres and attach the petals and centres to a cone-shaped piece of pink clay, using the cocktail stick. Attach more flowers directly to her head. Place the bears next to each other so they are holding hands. Support the figures by leaning them against a cup whilst baking. Bake the cup and bears on a ceramic tile.

Student Bear

Materials:

Half a block of brown polymer clay for the whole bear

Black clay for the nose and mortar board

White clay for the diploma and a little blue for the ribbon

Two glass beads for eyes

A small length of black waxed cotton cord

Tools:

Polymer clay blade

Knitting needle

Half a wooden cocktail stick to support the head

Cocktail stick

Square cookie cutter

Pasta machine or roller

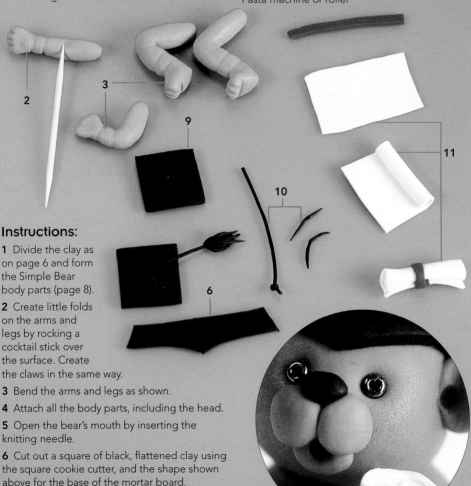

Instructions:

1 Divide the clay as on page 6 and form the Simple Bear body parts (page 8).

2 Create little folds on the arms and legs by rocking a cocktail stick over the surface. Create the claws in the same way.

3 Bend the arms and legs as shown.

4 Attach all the body parts, including the head.

5 Open the bear's mouth by inserting the knitting needle.

6 Cut out a square of black, flattened clay using the square cookie cutter, and the shape shown above for the base of the mortar board.

7 Attach the ears and create ear holes.

8 Place the base of the mortar board around the head.

9 Use the knitting needle to make a hole through the centre of the mortar board.

10 Form a knot at one end of the black waxed cord and thread the other end through the hole in the board. Form a knot at the other end and attach a ball of black clay. Roll out several tiny sausages of black clay and attach to the ball at the end. Attach the top of the board to the base.

11 Create the diploma by rolling up flat, white clay and wrapping a blue strip for a ribbon around it.

12 Place the diploma between his hands and seat the bear on a tile to bake.

This proud-looking bear would make a great gift for a graduating student.

Halloween Bear

Materials:

Green polymer clay for the face
and hands

Black clay for the cloak, arms,
hat and nose

Blusher and brush

Two shades of brown for the
broomstick

Two glass beads for eyes

Aluminium foil

Tools:

Polymer clay blade

Knitting needle

Half a cocktail stick to support the head, another
to create claws and folds and another for the broom

Pasta machine or roller

Ceramic tile

Instructions:

1 Form an armature out of the foil (see above).

2 Place a flattened scrap of black clay at the
base of the foil and another at the top, and insert
the half cocktail stick. This will be the body.

3 Create the head and ears (as on page 8) from
green clay and attach the head to the body.

4 Flatten black clay, cut out a cloak, and place it
around the foil.

5 Form the sleeves from black clay, as shown on the opposite page.

6 Create little green hands and insert them into the sleeves. Bend the arms and attach them to the body.

7 For the broomstick, flatten a piece of brown clay and wrap around a cocktail stick. Add a lump of yellow-brown clay to one end, then cover with lots of little sausage shapes of yellow-brown clay for the bristles.

8 For the hat, form a ball of black clay and ease out a tip. Pinch the base all round to form the brim. Attach it to the head.

9 Add a touch of blusher to the cheeks before baking. Make little whisker holes formed using the cocktail stick.

This spooky witch can come out every year for Halloween parties. The green clay adds a ghoulish touch to an otherwise cute bear.

Birthday Bear

Materials:

Pink polymer clay for the body

White for the snout and ball

A variety of colours for the ball

Dark pink for the nose

Two glass beads for eyes

Candle and holder

Tools:

Polymer clay blade

A cocktail stick to support the head and another to insert the glass beads

Knitting needle

Pasta machine or roller

Ceramic tile

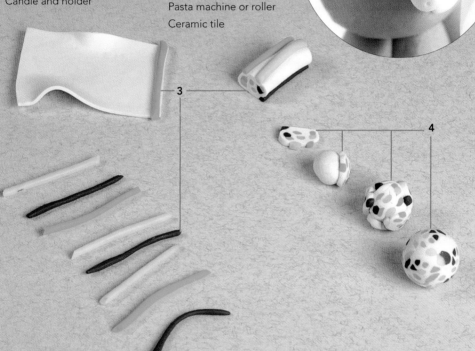

3

4

Instructions:

1 Create a Simple Bear from page 8, but add claws and folds using the cocktail stick and bend her arms.

2 Mould the paws around the candle holder to make an impression, then remove the holder before baking.

3 Create the little ball by flattening white clay and inserting little sausages of bright colours in between the folds as you roll up the flat white clay.

4 Cut off slices and place them around a ball of white, then roll between the palms of your hands to mould all the colours together.

The blue bear has been created using the *Simple Bear* instructions on page 8. His legs have been bent before attaching them to the body. Use the knitting needle to open his mouth. Remember to remove the candle holders before baking the bears. These cheerful little birthday bears could of course be made in sugarpaste to decorate a birthday cake.

Musician Bear

Materials:

Brown polymer clay for the body

Lighter brown clay for
the snout

Very light brown clay for the
recorder

Black clay for the nose

Tools:

Polymer clay blade

Cocktail sticks

Knitting needle

Pasta machine or roller

Ceramic tile

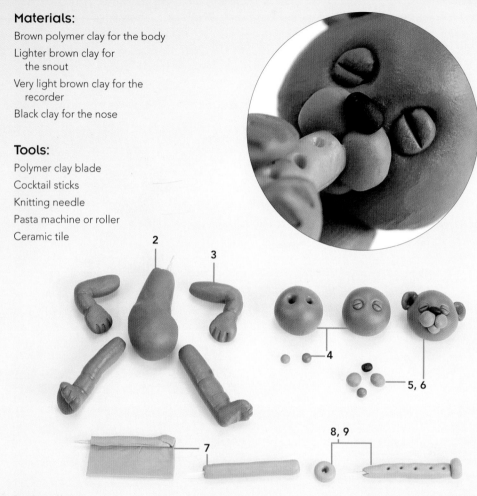

Instructions:

1 Create a Simple Bear from page 8, but make the legs long and thin and add claws and folds using the cocktail stick.

2 Squeeze the top of the body and roll gently between your finger and thumb to obtain the shape shown above.

3 Bend the arms ready to hold the recorder.

4 Create two eye sockets using the knitting needle and insert two balls of the same colour. Create the closed eyes by marking slits with the blade.

5 Add the snout and nose, then connect the head to the body.

6 Attach the ears and create ear holes with the knitting needle.

7 For the recorder, flatten the very light brown clay and wrap it around a cocktail stick. Leave a point sticking out at the end.

8 Make a tiny ball of the very light brown clay, squash it slightly, make a hole in the middle with the knitting needle and attach it to the end of the recorder.

9 Create the holes along the top using the knitting needle.

10 Insert the recorder into the bear's mouth and connect its paws to the recorder.

11 Position your bear on the tile ready for baking.

This gifted bear is in raptures as he plays his recorder. He would make a lovely present for a musical friend.

Christmas Bear

Materials:

Very light brown polymer clay for the top of the body

White clay for the snout, hat bobble and tissue paper

Black clay for the nose

Two glass beads for eyes

Red clay for the wrapping paper and hat

Green clay for the box

Tools:

Polymer clay blade

Pasta machine or roller

Two cocktail sticks

Knitting needle

Ceramic tile

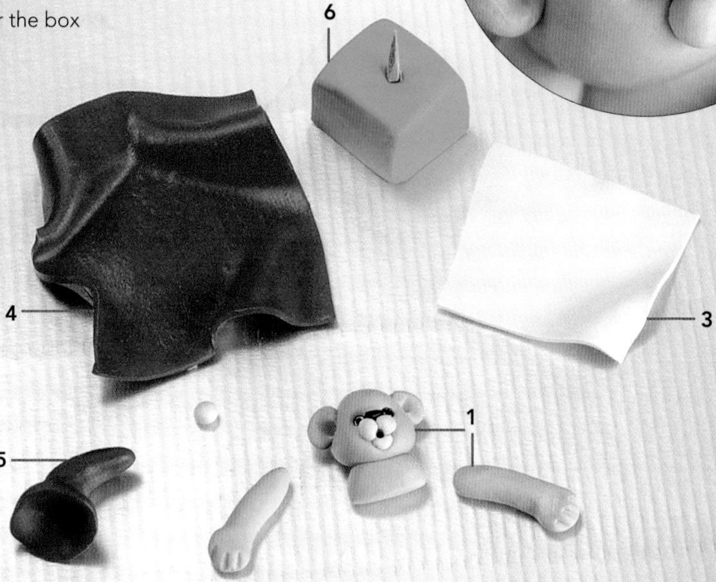

Instructions:

1 Create the top half of a bear and arms.

2 Form the green polymer clay into a box shape.

3 Flatten the white clay and cut into a square. Form the white bobble ready for the hat.

4 Flatten the red clay and cut into a larger square.

5 For the hat, first create a ball of red clay, then place your thumb at the base and ease it into the hat shape shown above.

6 Place half a cocktail stick in the green box, with the point facing upwards.

7 Lay the box on top of the red sheet and fluff up the red sheet to resemble paper.

8 Place the white sheet over the cocktail stick and fluff this up too.

9 Place the assembled half-bear over the protruding point of the cocktail stick.

10 Add the hat and bobble and for a surprised expression, use the knitting needle to open his mouth.

What better Christmas present than this bear bursting out of his gift box?
He would also make a lovely festive table decoration.

Native American Bear

Materials:

Brown polymer clay for the bear
A selection of colours for the jewellery
Black and white clay for the feather
Black for the nose
Two glass beads for eyes

Tools:

Polymer clay blade
Knitting needle
Cocktail sticks
Ceramic tile

Instructions:

1 Create the basic shapes of the Musician Bear (page 18), but this time bend the legs as well as the arms.

2 Create the jewellery by placing several thin strands of coloured polymer clay next to each other. Roll to join, and twist to create this candy-striped effect.

3 Assemble the bear and place him in position on the tile. Add the necklace before pushing the head into place.

4 Attach his little headband before attaching the ears above it.

5 Droop little dangly bits from the headband and add little balls of colour to resemble beads. Make little holes in the beads with the knitting needle.

6 For the feather, join a larger ball of black clay to a smaller ball of white, then ease into a feather shape. Create the impressions with the cocktail stick.

7 Add a small, coloured, flattened ball to the base of the necklace and create a hole with the knitting needle.

8 When you are satisfied with the bear's position, bake it.

The other bear is made from yellow clay and is sitting on a rock made from granite-coloured polymer clay with scrunched up aluminium foil inside to save using too much clay.

Dancing Bear

Materials:

Light brown polymer clay for the bear
White clay for the snout
Dark brown clay for the nose
Pink clay for the tutu and the bow
Two glass beads for eyes

Tools:

Polymer clay blade
Cocktail sticks
Knitting needle
Ceramic tile

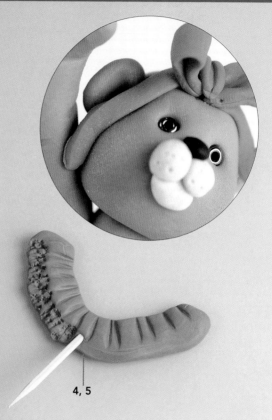

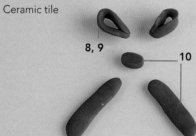

8, 9

10

4, 5

Instructions:

1 Follow the instructions for the Simple Bear (page 8) but make the arms and legs longer.

2 Assemble the bear, complete with the head, but do not attach the arms yet.

3 Place her on the tile, as it is easier to move the tile around than to pick her up.

4 Create a sausage shape out of the pink and create little creases using the knitting needle.

5 Break off a cocktail stick and with the rough broken end stab it many times, to create the ruffled effect.

6 Attach the tutu.

7 Now you can attach the arms.

8 To create the bow, roll out four little sausage shapes, then press with your fingers to flatten them.

9 Form loops from two of them and attach to the head.

10 Add the other two where shown, then add the little oval shape on top. Make a mark through the centre of the oval to create a crease. Bake in the oven.

Dancers will love these ballerina bears. The other little bear has larger ears placed further down the head. She also has a different-coloured snout and a brown nose. The lilac bow has been added to her blue tutu instead of placing it on her head. She has a matching choker made from a sausage shape of blue. A little ball of lilac has been added to the choker and a hole created through the centre using the knitting needle. Experiment with different body positions for these agile bears.

Panda

Materials:

Half a block of black
  polymer clay
Quarter block of white
A little pink
A little green
Two glass beads for eyes
Wet wipes

Tools:

Polymer clay blade
Cocktail sticks
Knitting needle
Ceramic tile

Note

When you are using
white along with darker
colours, always keep wet
wipes handy to prevent
contaminating the white.

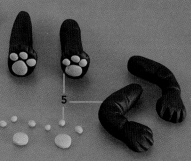

Instructions:

1 Shape the body from white clay
and insert half a cocktail stick to
support the head.

2 Form a ball of white for the head,
then add two tiny flattened balls of black for patches around the eyes. Add the black ears.

3 Create two eye sockets within the patches using the knitting needle and insert two tiny
balls of white for eyeballs. Insert the glass beads using a cocktail stick.

4 Add a little black chin followed by the two balls of black for the cheeks, then add a little
pink nose.

5 Create the arms and legs out of black clay as shown above, and add little balls of pink
clay for the pads. Create indentations with the cocktail stick for claws.

6 Flatten a small strip of black clay and wrap around the top of the body.

7 The panda is now ready to be assembled as shown opposite.

8 Create foliage out of green clay and place it in the panda's mouth using a cocktail stick.

9 Arrange your panda on the tile and make any adjustments needed before baking.

People who like more exotic bears will love this beady-eyed panda. Experiment with different poses or create a panda looking upwards by placing the beads towards the top of the white eyeballs. You will be surprised how this changes the character.

Fairy Bear

Materials:

Half a block of light blue
  polymer clay
A little dark blue clay
A little white clay
A little green clay
A little red clay
Two glass beads for eyes

Tools:

Polymer clay blade
Knitting needle
Cocktail sticks
Small star cookie cutter
Pasta machine or roller
Ceramic tile

2   3   4

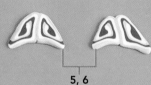

5, 6

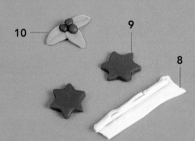

10   9

8

Instructions:

1 Follow instructions for the Simple Bear (page 8), but add little dark blue pads to the soles of the feet and create indentations for claws using a cocktail stick.

2 For the wings, flatten scraps of light blue, white and dark blue polymer clay, and place the sheets on top of each other as shown above. Trim to create a rectangular shape using a polymer clay blade.

3 Roll the flattened slices tightly.

4 Squeeze the roll to create a point at the top, so it becomes a triangular shape.

5 Remove four slices, (two for each wing.) Use the sharp polymer clay blade to ensure a clean cut.

6 Place two slices beside each other and squeeze gently to join. I have pinched out two points at each end, but this is optional.

7 Secure the wings to the back of the bear.

8 For the wand, wrap a flattened sheet of white polymer clay around a cocktail stick.

9 Cut out two dark blue star shapes, then sandwich the wrapped cocktail stick between them.

10 Shape some tiny leaves out of the green clay and place on the bear's head. Add little balls of red clay for berries. Bake on a tile.

The second little bear is an angel, and has green and white wings which I have fanned out to create a different shape. His ears are smaller and his nose bigger. I have positioned him kneeling in prayer.

Wizard Bear

Materials:

Scrap clay that has been twisted for the cloak

Mid-brown polymer clay for the head and hands

White for the eyeballs, star and the tip of the wand

Black for the nose

Blue for the hat and light blue for the wand, with two little scraps of red clay

Two glass beads for eyes

Tools:

Polymer clay blade

Pasta machine or roller

Knitting needle

Small star cookie cutter

Cocktail sticks

Aluminium foil

Ceramic tile

Instructions:

1 This time I have used a different style for the head. Begin by creating a ball out of the brown clay, then ease out a snout.

2 Create two eye sockets using the knitting needle and insert two tiny balls of white clay for the eyeballs. Add the glass beads for pupils.

3 Shape the mouth like an upside down 'Y' using the cocktail stick and create little whisker holes.

4 Use the knitting needle to press dimples into the corners of the mouth.

5 Flatten the scrap polymer clay to create the cloak.

6 Follow the instructions for the Halloween Bear (page 14) to create the arms and hands.

7 The body armature is identical to that of the Halloween Bear. Do not forget to insert the half cocktail stick into the top of the armature to secure the head.

8 Create a long, thin sausage out of light blue clay for the wand, and wrap it around a cocktail stick. Add a little ball of red to the tip, then a ball of white followed by a larger ball of red, which you will need to form into a point.

9 Create the hat in the same way as for the Halloween Bear's, add a white star and bake.

This bear is just brimming with magic. Tiny changes can create a different look on a bear's face, and I have given this wizard a mystical expression.

Artist Bear

Materials:

Brown polymer clay for the bear
Black for the beret and nose
Beige for the palette
White for the eyeballs and paint splatters
A variety of colours for the paints
Two glass beads for eyes

Tools:

Polymer clay blade
Knitting needle
Cocktail sticks
Ceramic tile

6

4, 5

Instructions:

1 Use the guidelines for creating the Simple Bear (page 8). The difference here is that the snout and body are the same shade of brown, and white eyeballs have been added. Follow the instructions for eyeballs from the Wizard Bear on page 30.

2 Once the bear parts have been formed, add whisker holes and claws using a cocktail stick.

3 Seat your bear on the ceramic tile while you create his beret and paint palette.

4 For the paint palette, form a ball out of beige polymer clay. Flatten it and cut out the shape shown above.

5 For the paint splatters, soften several colours and press them firmly to your work surface. Using a cocktail stick, scrape away tiny lumps and attach them to the palette. Use the same technique to apply the paint splatters to this messy little bear's body.

6 To create the beret, form a ball out of black polymer clay and flatten it very slightly, then add the tiny sausage of black to the top using a cocktail stick. Place the finished beret on the bear's head.

7 Ensure that the bear's arms are connected to the paint palette before baking him. Have fun and experiment!

This messy bear would be a lovely gift for an artistic friend, or an art teacher.

Gypsy Bear

Materials:

Brown polymer clay for the bear
White for the eyeballs
Black for the nose and cloth
Purple for the shawl
Two glass beads for eyes
One large glass bead for the crystal ball
Jump rings for earrings

Tools:

Polymer clay blade
Knitting needle
Cocktail sticks
Pasta machine
    or roller
Ceramic tile

Instructions:

1 Use the Simple Bear instructions (page 8) to obtain the correct proportions. The difference here is that the bear is all one colour and does not have a white snout.

2 After forming the basic shapes, bend the arms and legs and create claws before fixing the arms and legs to the body.

3 To acquire a wide-eyed expression for this bear, you will need to create two nice, deep eye sockets using the knitting needle and insert a tiny white ball of clay in each. Place the beads for pupils towards the bottom, so that the white at the top becomes predominant.

4 Opening the mouth enhances this expression of surprise, so do this by inserting a knitting needle.

5 Attach the head to the body and attach two little balls of matching brown polymer clay for the ears. Squeeze them gently to flatten them, create the ear holes with the knitting needle, then cut two tiny slits and insert the jump rings for earrings. Squeeze gently to seal the join.

6 The shawl and black cloth are created by cutting flattened clay into the shapes shown and attaching to the bear before baking.

If you look at Baby Bear's blanket on page 44, you will see that I have used a scrap of lace to make a patterned impression on it. You could apply this to this bear's shawl.

Gardener Bear

Materials:

Mid-brown polymer clay for
    the bear

Black clay for the nose

Orange and green clay
    for carrots

Dark brown clay for the soil

Two glass beads for eyes

Tools:

Polymer clay blade

Knitting needle

Cocktail sticks

Pasta machine or roller

Ceramic tile

2

5

3

6

Instructions:

1 Create the bear using the Simple Bear instructions (page 8). I have squeezed his body in a little at the top so his belly is larger. His arms and legs are stumpy, giving him a more rustic appearance. I have pushed the eye beads a little further into the head so they appear deep-set. The Gardener Bear also has a bigger nose and an open mouth.

2 For the base, flatten a lump of dark brown clay and place it on the tile.

3 Place the bear on top of the brown clay, then take a further lump of dark brown clay, soften it, then poke it with the broken end of a cocktail stick to create texture so that it resembles soil.

4 Now he will need some carrots! Begin by rolling out several little balls of orange clay, then, one at a time, place your finger over one side of the ball and roll gently until a point is formed.

5 Once all the carrots have been formed, take a cocktail stick and roll the carrot gently back and forth, from base to tip to create little grooves.

6 Form little thin green sausages and bend them in half, then attach two to each carrot using the cocktail stick.

7 Attach a carrot to the bear's paw, then arrange the other carrots around him.

8 Bake on the tile at the recommended temperature.

This earthy bear clearly does not mind getting his hands dirty. Why not make him for a green-fingered friend?

Polar Bear

Materials:

Half a block of white
polymer clay
A little black clay
Two glass beads for eyes

Tools:

Polymer clay blade
Cocktail sticks
Knitting needle
Ceramic tile

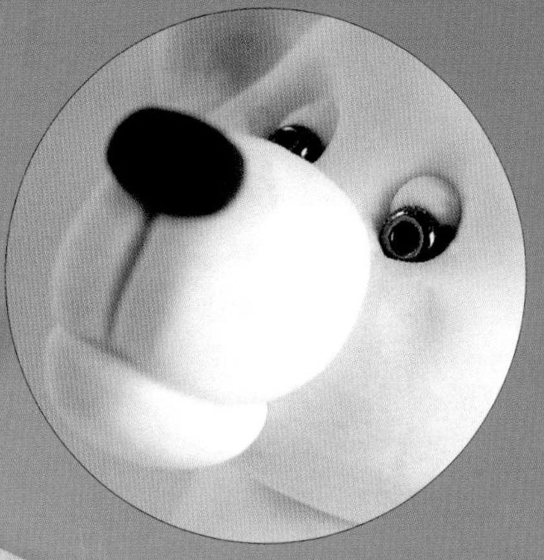

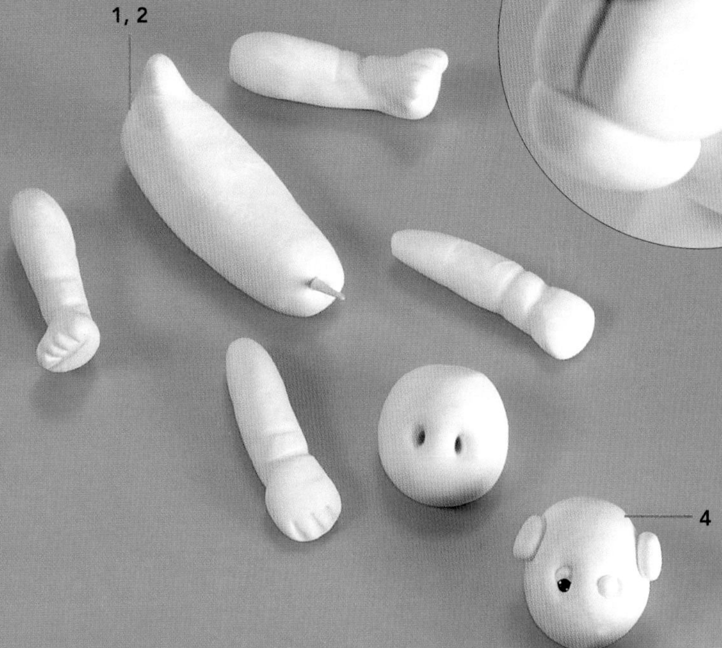

1, 2

4

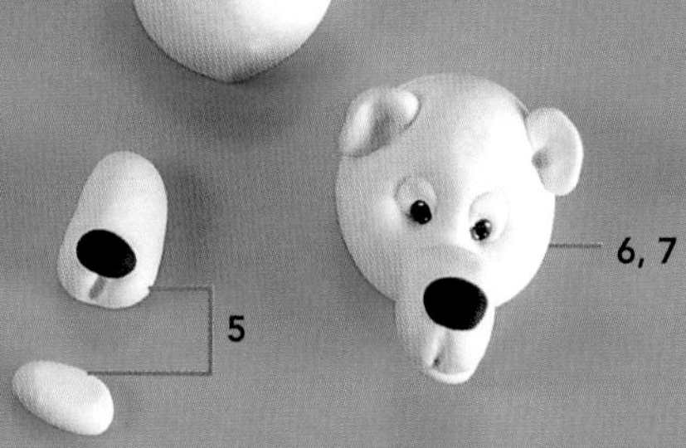

5

6, 7

Instructions:

1 Divide the clay as shown on page 6.
This time though, the body needs to be
shaped longer. It also needs a little stump
of a tail.

2 Form the shapes for the body and the back
and front legs as shown above. Insert the half
cocktail stick ready to support the head.

3 Attach the front and back legs.

4 Form a ball for the head, then create two eye sockets using the
knitting needle. Insert two tiny balls of white clay into each, then add
the glass beads.

5 The snout is created out of two lumps of white clay. For the top part,
form a short, fat white sausage shape. Push it firmly on to the head.

6 Use a cocktail stick to create a vertical crease, then add a smaller ball of clay beneath it to form a mouth.

7 Add a nice big, black nose and little white ears.

8 Attach the head to the body and bake on the tile.

The other polar bear is sitting up, making snowballs. A little blusher applied to his face adds a touch of life.

DIY Bear

Materials:

Half block of mid-brown polymer clay for the bear

A lighter brown for the snout

White for the eyeballs

Black for the nose and hammer head

Scraps of varying shades of brown for the planks and the hammer handle

Two glass beads for eyes

Tools:

Polymer clay blade

Knitting needle

Cocktail sticks

Three dress-making pins

Pasta machine or roller

Ceramic tile

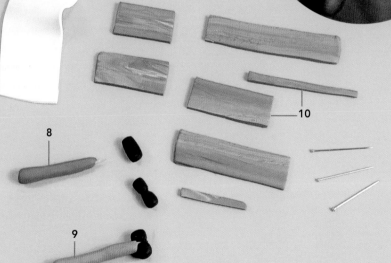

8

9

10

Instructions:

1 Begin by dividing the clay as for the Simple Bear (page 6).

2 When shaping this bear, make the arms and legs long enough so that you can bend them.

3 Create folds and claws using the cocktail stick, and assemble the body.

4 Create eye sockets for this bear, to give him an air of concentration.

5 Insert tiny balls of white into the sockets, then place the beads towards the base, so it appears as though he is looking down, concentrating on his work.

6 Attach the head, then the ears.

7 I have used dress-making pins as nails, so insert two into his mouth. (This is not recommended in real life, but this little detail adds humour to the scene!)

8 To create the hammer, cover a cocktail stick with a layer of flattened, light brown polymer clay, but leave the point sticking out at the end.

9 Create the hammer head as shown in the photograph opposite, attach to the pointed end and place it in the bear's paw.

10 The planks are simple to create. Mix a few shades of brown together to obtain a marbled effect, and flatten them using the pasta machine or roller. Create the grain by running the point of a cocktail stick gently over the surface. Cut into strips.

11 Arrange the bear on the tile surrounded by the planks of wood and bake at the recommended temperature.

For the other little bear, flatten some white clay, to resemble wallpaper, and drape it over the little bear's body. Use your imagination and approach the task with a sense of humour!

Toy Bear

Materials:

Brown polymer clay for the bear

Dark brown for its nose, ear inserts and pads

A contrasting brown for eyeballs

Two glass beads for eyes

Tools:

Polymer clay blade

Knitting needle

Cocktail sticks

Ceramic tile

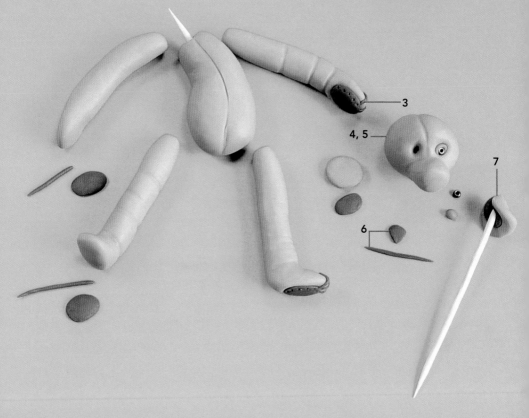

Instructions:

1 Divide the polymer clay into four equal sections. Unlike the Simple Bear (page 8), the arms on the Toy Bear are the same length as the legs. So one quarter of the clay will be divided into two for the legs; the second quarter is for the body; the third is cut in half to create the arms and the fourth is for the head and ears.

2 Create the body parts as shown opposite. This bear needs to look floppy, so ensure its arms and legs are long and dangly.

3 Add little pads of flattened dark brown clay for the pads on all the paws. Use the cocktail stick to create little holes to resemble stitching. Attach to the paws.

4 For the head, ease out a snout from a ball of brown clay and scratch the surface, to resemble a seam, using the cocktail stick.

5 Create two eye sockets and insert a contrasting shade of brown for the eyeballs. Add the two tiny glass beads.

6 Using thin strands of dark brown clay, form an upside down 'Y' shape for the mouth, then add a triangular nose.

7 For the ears, form two small balls of brown, squash slightly, then make two flattened smaller balls of the dark brown. Stick the dark brown to the lighter brown, then insert the finished ears using the cocktail stick.

8 Attach the head and arrange your bear on the tile to be baked. Try to get the general feeling of how a toy bear would sit. A good idea is to find your own bear or ask someone if you can borrow theirs, then observe how it sits. Experiment and enjoy!

Toy Bear is an old-fashioned teddy bear who looks as though he has been thoroughly cuddled over the years. The little lilac bear, his friend from the toy box, has been created using the same proportions but has decided to lie down.

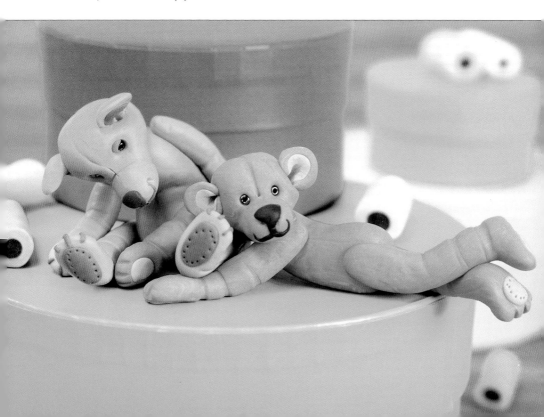

Baby Bear

Materials:

Brown polymer clay for the bear

White for the snout

Black for the nose

Light blue for the blanket

Aluminium foil

Scrap of lace or paper doily

Tools:

Polymer clay blade

Knitting needle

Cocktail stick

Pasta machine or roller

Ceramic tile

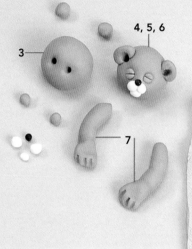

Instructions:

1 Create an armature for the body out of aluminium foil. The body will be covered by the blanket, so you do not need to make it out of clay.

2 The blanket is made by softening then flattening light blue polymer clay. Use a scrap of lace or paper doily to create an impression, then cut the blanket into a triangular shape large enough to wrap around the bear.

3 For the head, form a small ball out of the brown clay. Create two eye sockets with the knitting needle.

4 Insert two tiny balls of clay the same colour as the head.

5 Use the polymer clay blade to cut two tiny slits to make it appear as if the bear is sleeping.

6 Add the chin, cheeks and little nose, then add the ears.

7 Create the little arms and make impressions for claws using the cocktail stick.

8 Attach the head to the foil, then the arms, and wrap the baby snugly in the blanket.

9 Place on the ceramic tile and bake at the recommended temperature.

Mummy and baby bear have been created using the Simple Bear instructions (page 8), but with eye sockets and white eyeballs. They also have little pads on their feet.

The twin baby girl bears have a white sheet beneath them made from flattened white clay, and a pink blanket to cover them.

Valentine's Bear

Materials:

Two shades of brown polymer clay
  for the bears
Darker brown for the noses
Two glass beads for eyes
Pink and green for the rose

Tools:

Polymer clay blade
Knitting needle
Cocktail sticks
Ceramic tile

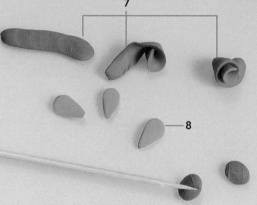

Instructions:

1 Create the bears' bodies using the
Simple Bear instructions (page 8).

2 For the lighter brown bear, bend the arms and legs and create claws using the
cocktail stick.

3 Like Baby Bear (page 44), this little fellow has closed eyes, so create sockets with the
knitting needle and insert two tiny balls the same colour as the bear. Create two slits.

4 Add the snout and nose, which are also the same colour as the body, and attach the head
and ears.

5 For his little friend, bend her arms and create claws using the cocktail stick. Leave the
legs straight.

6 Place the two together on the ceramic tile while you create the rose and fallen petals.

7 Flatten a strip of pink clay, then roll it, as shown above, to create the rose. Create little
fallen petals by forming lots of pink balls and flattening them.

8 Create three small green balls and pinch them at the ends to form the leaves.

9 Now for the fun part, which is adding the rose and petals and ensuring the two bears look
happy together. Bake on the tile at the recommended temperature.

These romantic bears would make a lovely Valentine's or engagement gift.

You are invited to visit the author's website:
www.birdyheywood.com

Acknowledgements
Special thanks to my children and grandchildren, who have provided me with inspiration and love.